10 Secrets to Marketing Success Through Analytics

1. Why Analytics Is Essential for Marketing Success

Studying the metrics of what you do is a very important part of having a successful business. Without looking at the numbers you really cannot know exactly why you experienced either success or failure. You can make assumptions, but when you don't have to do that it's better to use facts to ensure that your efforts aren't a waste.

* If You Can't Measure It Doesn't Exist – When you set goals, they should be something that can be expressed in numbers: clicks, page views, sign-ups, buys and so forth. You can even assign values to conversions so that Google Analytics tells you what a particular conversion is worth to you without you having to leave the system.

* Help You Get to Know Your Visitors – You probably set up a certain idea of your audience before you even started your business. You created marketing materials based on your ideal audience and it's worked. But, can it

work better? If you dig deep into your audience's demographics (especially the people who've converted), you most certainly can.

* You'll know What Content Is Most Important – When you set up analytics you can see what blog posts, articles, and other content is getting more traction. You can see views, comments, and more, which can help you judge better what type of content you need to create more of.

* Lets You Understand Top Referrers – Using the data you collect; you can find out who/what is sending the most traffic (converted traffic) to your website. This is useful because if it's one particular person (like an affiliate) or one website, you can give them some extra love to encourage more of the same.

* Helps You Study Your Competition – Nothing is more important outside of your visitors than your competition. You can learn a lot from your competition when you can get to know everything they are doing - including the keywords they use, the prices they charge for their products, and even their conversion rates.

* Teaches You What Works for Your Audience – When you study your numbers you can find out if the ideas you've had work or not. Some will, some won't. You can find out what works, optimize it and do more of it by looking at the data.

* Enables You to Kill Projects That Fail – You don't even have to allow projects to continue if the numbers show that they are failing all the way around. You can kill projects fast when you're doing them online. It's not like the old days when you had to let things run their course and watch your money go down the drain.

Running your business by the numbers is something that can really help advance it in ways that you may not have previously considered. It's imperative to learn about metrics, goal setting, and how to determine correlation, because not everything is always as it seems when it comes to the numbers.

2. A/B Testing with Google Analytics

A/B testing consists of having two versions of whatever you're testing that are very slightly different. You then divide the traffic between the two versions and see which one converts at a higher rate. It seems simple enough, but most marketers don't even do it, even though it has shown time and again that website owners who conduct proper A/B testing experience higher conversions and a higher return on investment than those who don't.

Create the Marketing Collateral

Whether it's a sales page, newsletter landing page or something else entirely, create the designs in twos. You want to create two landing pages (A and B) that are slightly different. For example, perhaps each page has a different image on it, or a different headline, or perhaps a different buy/call to action button.

Upload the Pages to Your Site

You'll need the URLs of the pages that you want to test. Make sure when you collect the URLs that you name each test page so that you know which one each URL is assigned to. Keep track of it all to ensure that you don't get mixed up, so that your results will turn out accurately.

Set Your Goals

Obviously, your goal is to make more money and increase your return on investment. But you will have many different conversion goals, such as newsletter sign-ups, freebie downloads, sales and more. Choose an "experimental objective" within Google Analytics to create your goals. You can find this under Behavior and Experiments. Just click "Create Experience" to get started.

Name Your Experiment

Choose names for your experiments so that you can identify which page is working best during the testing. Once you've done this you can set your goals under "objectives for this experiment". You have several choices such as AdSense, ecommerce, and many other goal metrics. Choose the best one for your test.

Run the Test

Once you have it all set up and uploaded, you can let it run. Keep checking up on your statistics as often as you can; at first you may want to do it daily, then maybe weekly. Let it run long enough that you're positive on which test, A or B, worked better.

Pick the Best Conversion Page

Remember that conversions and clicks are nice, but money is the point. There are always possibilities that the most clicked and trafficked page is not the one that makes the most money. Therefore, it's imperative to run the experiment long enough with enough variables to notice. For example, don't sign people up for the same list even if the series is the same; that way you know which list is filled with either A or B respondents.

When you know what your goals are, and test to find out how accurate you have been designing sales pages and landing pages for your audience, you'll soon get better at converting and making more money. Testing with Google Analytics is free and well worth it.

3. Using Analytics to Understand Your Visitors

Your website visitors are much more than page views. They are people that take various actions (or not) when they get to your site. It's important to understand as much as you can about them. Due to Google's powerful network they have a lot of information on your users. You may as well use it to get to know your real audience.

* Who Are They? – Knowing exactly who your visitors are is useful because when you first choose your audience you are usually just making a guess on the best audience so that you can create marketing materials and products and services. But, once you have your site live and your products selling, checking up to ensure that you're still marketing to the right people helps tremendously.

* Where Did They Come From? – How your audience finds you is an important thing to know. Because if your audience is finding you more from one location over another, you need to up your activities there so you can get

more of that traffic. In Google Analytics you can find this information under All Referrals.

* Where Is Your Audience Located? – You can use the Geo Location area of analytics to find out where your audience lives. Even if you're marketing worldwide it's good information to have, because the location of your audience does help you make some assumptions about their personalities and values.

* What Do They Do on Your Site? – You can map what each visitor does on your site so that you can see which menu items are most popular. This can help you determine what type of content you should put more of on your website. Put more of what they're reading and viewing on your site to attract even more visitors like them.

* What Do They Want? – By analyzing where they go, how they interact and so forth, you can make some assumptions about what they want from you. If they're reading blog posts, do more; if they watch and share videos more often, do more of that.

* Where Are Their Conversion Paths? – Knowing the steps, a user takes to reach a

buying decision is important, because it can help you create paths that work for your visitors based on the conversions already made. This information can help you optimize your sales funnels.

* What Information Do They Comment On? – If you have a forum, or have opened comments on your blog, or get emails from people who purchased something from you, what information do they comment on most? Is it positive, negative or indifferent? With that information, you can create more content that gets bigger responses.

Any information you can get on your visitors will help you improve not only your website, but your entire business. You can learn so much by what the current visitors do and don't do on your website. Use the information to make everything better and more targeted.

4. Using Analytics to Understand Your Competition

The more you can understand your competition, the better business you're going to have. You can learn so much from them - especially if they've been around longer than you have. If you know for a fact the competition is profitable and that they are good at what they do, it's even more important to learn all you can from them. You can do that by using analytics.

* Google Alerts – This is an excellent, free service. Sign in and choose keywords, names, and more to search for. Then, set up how often you want to receive the alerts in your email inbox. You can scan each email to find information about your competition that you can use in your own business.

Link - https://www.google.com/alerts

* Social Mention – Use this cloud-based search engine to search websites, blogs and more for mentions about your competition. Then you can go take a look at what they're doing. Identify the gaps in their offerings and you can outshine your competition in no time.

Link - http://socialmention.com/

* Website Grader – While it does ask for your website and not your competition's (and your email address), you can still use it to check the health of someone else's website. The information you will receive is page size, page speed, redirects and more, including how many requests for the site have been made. It also tells you how they're doing on SEO and more.

Link - https://website.grader.com/

* Link-Assistant.com – Using this downloadable software you can study keywords of your competitor's site so that you will know what keywords they're using. You can then use them on your own website to nab their traffic.

Link - http://www.link-assistant.com/

* SocialAdNinja – You can use this software to copy and make your competitor's ads your own. Of course, you don't copy them exactly, as you are selling your own products, but this will help you duplicate the most successful ads online.

Link - http://www.socialadninja.com/

* KeywordSpy – This software is an amazing way to profit from your competition's hard work and research. You can find out what keywords they're using, what they're spending for AdWords, their ROI estimate, and much more.

Link - http://www.keywordspy.com/

* Open Site Explorer by MOZ – You can get a lot of information about your competition from this cloud-based option. You can get information about the links that come into the site and the anchor text used, and you can even compare five sites. What's more, it's free when you sign up.

Link - https://moz.com/researchtools/ose/

Using these tools to discover important data to analyze about your competition is a great way to grow your business and please your audience. By keeping an eye on your competition, you can learn about what your audience really wants and what they really respond to.

5. Using Analytics to Plan Where Your Business Is Going

Analytics can tell you what happened, why it happened, what will happen and how you can make it happen. "It" consists of any goal that you've set for your business. Using analytics to inform you about these issues will help you make your business even more prosperous. The insights you get from the data are immeasurably useful for business owners today. They will help you guide all your actions.

* Operate a Better Business – When you use data to help you learn about your business, your competition, where you stand and where you want to go, you'll truly end up with a better business than you ever thought possible. Today, data can actually be predictive and almost give you directions on what to do next to boost your business and make it better.

* Be More Innovative – As you look at the data you have, and you can see what happened

and how it happened, you can take that information to repeat whatever worked so that you can get more good results out of it. But, you can also use that same data to add complementary products and services to your offerings or even change direction altogether.

* Stay Ahead of Trends - Think of Netflix's decision making. Had they minded their data when they thought they were going to stream only, they would have known in advance that this idea wasn't ready to work - although it probably will in the future as people who use electronics instead of digital devices will become fewer and fewer.

* Face Challenges – Every business face challenges, and you can even predict some by looking at data. For example, some businesses are seasonal in nature, even though in some cases there is no reason for them to be seasonal. But if you check the data you might find that your business has times where you make more sales. You can use that information to pump up advertising during the off season.

* Information to Help You Grow – Analytics can help you get to know your audience even better. When you first start a business, you choose almost out of thin air who you want to

be your target audience. You set up all your advertising and marketing with that in mind. But, you might find through analytics that you have a far different audience than you thought. This can help you narrow down and optimize your marketing materials so that you can grow your business.

If you want to grow your business and plan exactly where it's going, use analytics to discover insights into your business that will help you accomplish that goal. Predictive analytics can help you make the right decision for your business.

6. Using Analytics to Improve Your Website

Website analytics are there to help you track and measure various parameters of your website. But, they can also help you ensure that your website is completely optimized in every aspect - including layout, speed, SEO, and more. For example, with Google Analytics you can create many different reports to help you understand the health of your website.

Set Goals First

The first thing to do is set goals for your analytics. For example, if you are having a webinar you might want to study how many people sign up for your webinar and signed up for your newsletter. If you've created a white paper you may want to keep track of how many people downloaded the white paper, and if you put links inside the white paper you want to know how many people click through.

* Did SEO Work or Not? - Using the analytics that you have available; you can find out if

traffic or conversions increased after you updated your SEO on your site and added more content.

* What Type of Content Works Best? - You can also find out which posts are more popular, and which converted. When you take stock of which blog posts are popular, what do they have in common?

* Which Segments of Your Audience Convert at a Higher Rate? – If you use audience segmentation you can find out the segments that covert at a higher rate, which means you can then use that information to target that segment harder.

* What New Products or Services You Should Offer – When you determine through analytics what your visitors like most, you can offer complementary products or services, and even new things that they might like based on the data you collect.

* Help You Determine New Goals – As you research the data and information that you find in your analytics software, you can actually come up with new ideas for new goals - goals that you might not have come to if you hadn't

looked at the other data. For example, your first goal might be to get people to subscribe to your newsletter, and then you may set up a goal that people on your newsletter list convert to joining your membership site.

* Help You Choose the Right Keywords – One thing that Google Analytics and AdWords are really good at is helping you choose the right keywords. Plus, once you download a couple hundred keyword ideas it will also help you decide what type of content to add based on the keyword research.

* Help You Identify a Slow Loading Site – Sometimes website designers add too many interesting features that cause a website to slow down. If your website is too slow, visitors will leave, and Google will downgrade your website. By keeping tabs on this metric, you can take steps to improve.

Using analytics to help you improve your website is a great use of the software. You can ensure that your site is up to date, works fast, and has proper navigation and SEO so that you can convert visitors to buyers in no time.

7. Using Analytics to Detect Fraud

One of the most dreaded forms of fraud on the net is click fraud. It costs marketers and advertisers an enormous amount of money each year. Thankfully, you can discover click fraud and protect yourself if you know how. It's important to do so since click fraud is more than a five-billion-dollar business.

How Many Clicks from the Same IP Address?

Check to find out how long the clicks have been coming from the same IP address, and compare that to all your other clicks to find out if it's possible that it's click fraud. If you check enough, you'll know the pattern for your own website and know when something is wrong so you can block that particular IP address when needed (if it's a static IP address). You can find this information in your server's log.

Use a Service Like ClickReport.com

With this service you can find out a lot of information about your PPC activity that you need, such as date, time, IP address, location, keywords and much more. This is a great way to protect your investment in pay-per-click marketing. So much is lost in click fraud so it's great that you can protect yourself a little better with this service.

Test against Established Parameters

A good example for this to help a lot is to make sure your data entry is accurate. Don't allow people to input false answers in your forms. For example, if your form requires an address, don't allow them to put in all 9's for the zip code. Conversely, you can pull all data with invalid zip codes, check them out further and delete them and block static IPs if you believe they're fraudulent accounts.

Find Weaknesses in Your System

When you regularly study analytics, patterns emerge and when that happens you can figure out what is causing the issues if there is one. You always need some sort of proof when fraud is happening, and the proof is in the data that you have access to and can study.

Analytics Helps Detect and Prevent Fraud

Analytics offer a means by which to detect fraud and even alert you to a problem. If you set up any type of analytics system correctly - even Google AdWords - you can often detect fraud and put a stop to it as soon as possible.

It's important to do all that you can to stop and prevent fraud. It can affect your profits in enormous ways. It can even cause the ruin of an entire business. But if you use analytics to detect fraud you can be one of the smart business owners who lowers the damage that it can cause by catching them.

8. Social Media Analytics

One thing that is hard to do sometimes is to interpret what actions mean on social media. The fact is, not all actions even matter. It's important to know what matters and what doesn't. It's also important to know what everything means or potentially means based on other factors and the goals you set. Below are some important questions to consider.

* Leads – How many new leads did you get from the action you performed? If you set up a freebie guide and marketed that, how many people signed up and downloaded it? If people downloaded a freebie, how many who did that took further action?

* Engagement – When you make a post, how many people respond in some way to the engagement? What was the point of the engagement? Did the audience do what you thought they'd do?

* Reach – How many people shared your post? How far did the post reach, meaning how many people laid eyes on it and shared it?

If a lot of people shared it, you might consider adding more content like that.

* Impressions – When you boost a post on Facebook, how many impressions did it make versus how many people saw it, shared it, and engaged with it? What did they do afterwards?

* Funnels – With your analytics software you can set up a means to testing out your funnels to find out which type of funnel works best. This can help you identify holes in your plans to reach your goals.

* Unique Visits – It's important to know how many unique visits you get each day, where they came from, and what they did after they got there. Did they convert? Did they sign up for anything? Did they download something? Did they search your site?

* Repeat Visits – Having a lot of repeat visitors is a sign of a healthy site with a lot of content for the audience to read and look at. What is the percentage of repeat visitors versus new traffic? If it's low, what can you change? Are you targeting your audience correctly?

* Bounces – Are people coming to your website and then leaving before doing anything? If this rate is high, then that means something is wrong. Find out where the links are coming from and try to determine if the content is badly targeted or not.

* Exits – How and what page are people using to exit your website, and if they came from social media where did they come from? Can you pinpoint what is making them leave? What you can do to encourage them to stay or to convert them in some way, for example by using an exit pop-under?

* Time on Site – How long are your visitors staying on your page and what exactly are they doing while they are there? What do they read the most? What do they watch the most? What exactly are they doing that keeps them on the social media site? If they're only there a short time, what did they do?

* Growth – How fast are the visitors to your social media page/platform improving each month? Is it going up or down? What actions affect growth? How can you do more of those things to keep growing your website and your influence?

* Response – When you create a post, how long does it take your audience to respond and what type of responses do you get? Are they commenting, liking, sharing, retweeting and so forth?

* Inbound Links – How many others are sharing your social networks and causing people to link to your social media networks? Who is sharing your platform more and why?

Finally, the only thing that really matters in the scheme of things is conversions. If you're not meeting your conversion goals, then you need to readjust. Remember that conversions are what you determine that they are. You may be tracking email sign-ups, clicks or sales. It's up to you what a conversion means.

9. Nine Common Analytics Mistakes

If you truly want to improve your business, get more customers and make more sales, then you need to mind your numbers. The metrics behind what is working or not working is very important. They say that only 20 percent of your actions make up 80 percent of the results. What if you're working on the wrong 20 percent? If you study analytics, you're going to be so much more likely to work on the right 20 percent.

Below are nine common analytics mistakes. Hopefully by reading them you'll avoid making the same mistakes yourself.

1. Not looking at the Numbers at All — Many people have perfectly successful online and offline businesses where they never look at a single number. One might wonder what the point is if you're already successful. But the fact is, how much more successful can a business owner be if they know what's working and what's not working?

2. Looking at the Wrong Information – Many new people study information that really doesn't matter. For example, are "bounces" really bounces? Or, did they get taken to a redirect affiliate link that cannot be tracked via your analytics software?

3. Not Setting Up the Software Correctly – If you're new and you have no idea about the capabilities of the software or how to use it, you need to get training or have someone who is a professional set it up and give you reports. The software only works as well as the user.

4. Not Monitoring Regularly – Often, people spend a lot of time and money to set up analytics, but they never look at them again. This is terrible use of the software and a huge mistake for the business. Once you set it up, ensure that you monitor everything on a set schedule so that you will not miss anything.

5. Not Segmenting for Retargeting/Remarketing – One of the most powerful forms of marketing today is retargeting or remarketing to people who have visited your websites or had some sort of interaction before. Some people need to see your offerings multiple times in order to finally trust you. Don't miss out on this amazing ability.

6. Not Setting Conversion Goals – If you don't set goals within your software, you won't know if what you're trying to achieve is happening or not. You can make assumptions based on income, but you won't really know what's helping or hurting you.

7. Not Filtering Out Invalid Traffic – A lot of traffic can just mess up your numbers, so you need the ability and knowledge of how to filter out that particular traffic. The invalid traffic are people who visit your website to work, like yourself and your virtual assistant or web designer.

8. Not Setting Up Multiple Views – When you get reports, instead of trying to look at everything at once, set up multiple views so you can see what each parameter means to your business.

9. Not Differentiating the Types of Traffic – There are several types of traffic such as referral, direct and so forth. You should differentiate each type of traffic so that you know what is causing a spike in bounces or conversions.

If you're not using your analytics software properly due to lack of knowledge or time, consider hiring a professional. Google Analytics offers certification and a Google Badge for those who have passed the tests. If you do have time, consider going through the course yourself.

10. Nine Analytics Tools You Can Use

One of the most important things you can do as a business owner who uses internet marketing is to study the numbers. Some people think analytics is boring, but in truth it can be very exciting to find the key to unlock higher conversions and higher return on investment.

Here are nine different analytics tools you can use.

1. Chartbeat – This cloud-based software is a little different than some of the other products out there. This company realizes that clicks are only part of the story. With this software you'll know right away what content is working best on your website or blog.

Link - https://chartbeat.com/

2. Adobe Analytics – With this service you can gather deep insights in all your online activities, including mobile. Get to know each customer's journey inside and out from A to Z with just a few clicks. You can conduct a 360° customer analysis, use predictive intelligence and more.

Link - http://www.adobe.com/marketing-cloud/web-analytics.html

3. Google Analytics – This is the original free analytics software which is definitely worth trying out. It offers so many features and benefits that it would be impossible to go over them all in this space. But it would do your business good to learn it or hire a professional to help you with using the software.

Link - https://analytics.google.com/

4. Snowplow Analytics – This works on the idea of pipelines and with it you can view all customer interactions, monitor the performance of your business, and even respond to users in real time. You can track anything you want to track.

Link - http://snowplowanalytics.com/

5. Piwik – This is an open-source analytics tool that anyone can use. You and only you can see the information. You can self-host it or you can use it in the cloud. You're in full control of your tests and analytics.

Link - https://piwik.org/

6. Clicky – Almost a million websites use Clicky to monitor their web analytics in real time. If you want to know how your website is performing in a simple way, this software works wonders to help you make the right choices.

Link - https://clicky.com/

7. KissMetrics – The analytics you can get from KissMetrics will help you become more customer centric as you learn what makes your customers tick. You'll be able to optimize pages through testing and more. If you want to keep happy clients, this is great software to try.

Link - https://www.kissmetrics.com/home/

8. Woopra – You can use this software to track anonymous website and mobile app users even before they identify themselves and then after too. If you really want to get a good understanding of your customers and their buying cycle, try this software.

Link - https://www.woopra.com/

9. HubSpot Analytics – HubSpot offers an enormous amount for website owners and business owners in terms of analytics. The reports offer sales and marketing data in one spot for easier understanding.

Link - http://www.hubspot.com/products/analytics

Which software you choose to use depends on what your goals are. Plus, it depends on your own understanding and expertise when it comes to using the software. You might consider hiring a professional who is an expert in any of these software options so that you can get the most out of analytics.

www.ingramcontent.com/pod-product-compliance
Lightning Source LLC
Chambersburg PA
CBHW040255220526
45473CB00001B/484